WHEN THE MOVIES BEGAN:
First Film Stars

❖❖❖❖❖❖❖❖❖❖❖❖❖❖❖❖❖❖

by
Edgar Marvin

Illustrated by
Meredith Nemirov

cpi
contemporary perspectives, inc.

This book is distributed by Silver Burdett Company, Morristown, New Jersey 07960.

Library of Congress Number: 78-15167

Art and Photo Credits

Cover photos, Culver Pictures
Photos on pages 7 and 39, UPI
Photos on pages 9 and 11, Globe Photos
Photo on page 21, Photoworld
Photos on pages 26, 40, and 43, Culver Pictures
Every effort has been made to trace the ownership of all copyrighted material in this book and to obtain permission for its use.

Library of Congress Cataloging in Publication Data

Marvin, Edgar, 1924-
    When the movies began.

    SUMMARY: Norma Talmadge relates how she became an actress in the fledgling motion picture industry.
    1. Talmadge, Norma, 1897-1957 — Juvenile literature. 2. Moving-picture actors and actresses — United States — Biography — Juvenile literature. [1. Talmadge, Norma, 1897-1957. 2. Actors and actresses] I. Title.
PN2287.T15M3   791.43′028′0924   [B] [92]
ISBN 0-89547-055-1   78-15167

Manufactured in the United States of America
ISBN 0-89547-055-1

Contents

❖ Chapter 1 ❖

On Camera with Shaun Cassidy

It was a dark and windy night in October. The big clock in the church bell tower chimed 12 times. The old frame house on Elm Street was still and quiet. The Henderson family was fast asleep.

A man dressed in black moved across the wide porch. He tried the door. It was locked. Using a thin iron bar, he silently worked at the wood around the lock until he could pry open the door. He slipped inside and padded in soft shoes across the kitchen floor into the long, dark hall.

Seeming to know just where he was going, the stranger moved quickly into the living room. He pointed the beam of a small flashlight at Mr.

Henderson's desk. His gloved hand went to just one desk drawer on the left. He took out a thick folder of papers. He smiled. He had found what he was looking for.

Suddenly, the living room lights went on. A dog started barking. Startled and blinded by the bright light, the man in black turned and ran for the front door. With lightning speed Joe Hardy was on him, wrestling him to the floor.

"Cut!" a voice crackled from the darkened part of the room. "We'll have to take that again after lunch. Be back on the set at 1:30 everybody," called the director. The quiet television sound stage at Universal Studios in Universal City, California, suddenly became noisy and active. Actors, cameramen, directors, producers, and make-up people moved from the set to eat a hurried lunch. Shaun Cassidy and his co-star Parker Stevenson, known to millions of TV fans as "The Hardy Boys," walked from their places on the stage.

Cassidy turned to see Lola Pearsons walking toward him. His hazel eyes widened and he broke into a smile. One hand moved to push his straight blond hair, and the other took Lola's outstretched hand. She was a friend and also one of the most important movie and TV news reporters.

Shaun Cassidy and Parker Stevenson in a scene from "The Hardy Boys."

"How about some lunch, Lola? We can talk *and* eat back in my dressing room." Shaun got a bright smile and a quick nod from Lola that said "lead the way."

He pushed the door open, and Lola entered a room that was even more beautiful than the living room set she had just seen. "Wow, what a dressing room!" was all she could think to say. Her eyes took it all in — large comfortable chairs, a sofa, and a TV set.

Lola sat down and began reading from some notes in a book she held on her lap. "Your mother is the Oscar award-winning film and TV star, Shirley Jones. Your father was the famous Broadway and TV star, Jack Cassidy. Your older half-brother is David Cassidy, the recording star who used to be the star of the hit TV series, 'The Partridge Family.' You have two younger brothers — Patrick, 16 and Ryan, 12. You graduated from Beverly Hills High School. You have two record albums that have sold over a million copies each, 'Shaun Cassidy,' and 'Born Late.' Your single records have all gone to the top of the charts, 'Da Doo Ron Ron,' 'That's Rock 'n' Roll,' and 'Hey Deanie.' You wrote five of the ten songs on your latest L.P."

Shaun suddenly stood up with his hands high in the air. "Hey, wait a minute, Lola," he said, grinning. "So far you're right. But you make me sound like a bunch of *numbers*. I'm 19 years old. I think I'm pretty normal. I have one big problem though. I have no

8

Shaun with his parents and brothers Ryan and Patrick, right.

time for *myself*. I'm busy from six in the morning until 11 at night. Between filming 'The Hardy Boys' all week, concerts on the weekends, recording dates, and writing music, I don't have much time for a personal life . . ."

Lola broke in before Shaun finished the sentence. "Yes, that's the price of being a superstar, Shaun. Most American youngsters your age would gladly trade places with you in a minute. In a single year you could earn over a million dollars!"

"Lola, a lot of it is great. But a lot more isn't. It's hard work and sometimes I wonder if it's all worth it. I *love* show business! I have to love it. I'm from a show business family. I grew up in Beverly Hills, California. The children of show business greats were all around me. Their parents were always visiting our house.

"I graduated from Beverly Hills High School in June, 1976. When I was in junior high school, I had a bit part in my mother's play — *On a Clear Day You Can See Forever*. Then I was in a movie called *Born of Water*, which was released in June, 1976.

"While still in high school, I had done some European concerts and TV. In fact, I was better known in Europe than I was in America. For example, my first record, 'Morning Girl,' was released in Europe in January, 1976. Almost overnight it became a hit.

10

A star of today, Shaun needs lots of energy for his concerts.

"When I came back to the United States, I tried out for the part of Joe Hardy in 'The Hardy Boys' and I won the part. Did you know I sang 'Da Doo Ron Ron' on one of the first shows? The record was released in America practically at the same time that the TV series started. The record became a smash hit, and seeing me on TV every week helped to sell it."

Shaun smiled broadly, "And the rest is, as they say in show business, *history!* You know, it's a funny thing. In some ways, having famous parents helped me to get started. It made it easier to see important record and TV people. But it also meant that I had to work twice as hard once I had the job. I always had to prove myself. I didn't want people saying that I got the job because I was Shirley and Jack Cassidy's son or David Cassidy's brother."

Lola smiled as Shaun talked about his show business beginnings. "Well, Shaun, you certainly are a household word all over the world, no matter whose son you are!"

Shaun made a sour face. "Yeah, a household word who can't even go on a date in public without being mobbed. A household word who often hides in his house like ... a prisoner! I can't list my own phone number."

Lola sat back and sighed. She knew that Shaun was much too young to know what life was like for the stars of show business long ago. All at once she knew the story she had to tell this handsome young superstar.

"Shaun, I know how hard your life seems these days. TV shows, records, and concerts can keep a young star pretty busy. But I think you might like to know what life was like for the stars of long ago. I don't mean when your own parents were starting out. I mean even long before *that* — when the movies had just been born. Let me tell you the story of one of the very first movie stars."

❖ Chapter 2 ❖

"Movies" That Don't Move

Her name was Norma Talmadge. In 1910 she was 14, growing up in Brooklyn, New York. Even at the age of 14 Norma loved to act. While her younger sisters played with dolls, Norma ran a circus. She would drag cats and dogs into the house every Friday afternoon. The cellar would be her circus tent and Norma was the ringmaster. Friends could come to her circus for five pennies.

Norma's mother loved helping Norma and her sisters put on a play or a circus. To the girls, their mother always seemed as young as they were. They never called her "mother." They called her by her first name — Peg.

Norma's mother and father were poor. The family had to make its own fun. In the same way that we sit down to watch a TV show, Norma's family would make their own shows.

Even though her family had very little, Norma had always dreamed of being in the movies. And one Sunday her mother said something that could make her dream come true.

"You know, Norma, you're so pretty we ought to get someone to take your picture. Let's get pictures taken of all the girls," Peg shouted. "Of course, all three," her father agreed. And that's when it started. The Talmadge family went to have pictures taken.

The photographer kept looking at Norma. He had never seen such a pretty young girl. When he had taken all their pictures and was being paid, he suddenly turned to Norma's father.

"Mr. Talmadge, I think you are silly to be paying me to take your daughter's picture. I know someone who would pay *you* to take her picture."

Norma could not believe what she was hearing. Her father only laughed. Surely the photographer was only joking. But the man went on to say he was quite serious. He thought Norma would be perfect for the slides that were shown with songs at the movies.

Those were the days when it cost only five cents to go to the movies. The movie houses were called "nickelodeons." Black and white pictures on film that moved were very new. And the movies were very

short — under ten minutes. So along with your five cent movie they showed you some slides and played the piano. The music was important. The movies and the slides had no sound.

This photographer thought that Norma would be perfect for those slides. And at three dollars a slide! Norma had never thought anybody could be paid so much for something that sounded so wonderful.

Norma started going to the photo studio every afternoon when school let out, plus Saturday mornings. They snapped pictures of her like crazy. And Norma kept count of every one. When the week ended she figured she had earned $300.

But when Norma went to pick up her check it was for just nine dollars. It seems there had been a little misunderstanding. Seeing her surprised look, the photographer asked what was wrong. When she told him, he took her hand in his and said, "Three dollars a *song*, Norma. That's what we meant. Not three dollars a slide. There are more than 30 slides for each song!"

"Oh." That was all Norma could say. Still, she was just 14, and she had cardboard in her shoes to cover the holes. So it was hard to be too sad at being handed nine dollars. Even when she expected $300.

Meanwhile, Norma's mother Peg was visiting every neighborhood nickelodeon to find out where

Norma's slides were being shown. Now that she had a job, Norma could treat them all. Peg and the girls would sit in the nickelodeon for hours.

The nickelodeon was just an empty store. It was a narrow room with a walk down the center and rows of wooden folding chairs on either side.

Norma loved seeing herself on slides — even if they didn't move. There she was on the screen. In one picture she sat next to a stream. In another, she walked along a mountain road.

And always, no matter where she was in those slides, a song was played on the piano. But while her sisters would begin to yell, "Norma . . . look, that's Norma!" she would wait for the real movie to start again. Then she would pretend that she was in the *moving* picture. In her mind she was the actress on the screen — crying or laughing, waving her arms, and never making a sound. *Her* words were the ones they printed at the bottom of the screen.

"It's so hard to believe there was a time when movies had no sound." Shaun asked questions of Lola, one after another. "Who were the actors — who were the stars? Were there many different movies? Were they . . . ?"

Lola began to laugh. "Hold on, Shaun. I'm just coming to that part of the story. But I will tell you one thing. A star wasn't a star as you would think of a Barbra Streisand today. For one thing, no one even knew their names!" Lola saw the surprise on Shaun's

Alice Calhoun was another "Vitagraph Girl" ▶ in the early days of the movies.

face. *"That's right, you never knew the name of the star you went to see in a movie."*

Norma's favorite star was known only as "The Vitagraph Girl." She played in movies that were made by a company called Vitagraph Studios. Norma also liked others. There was "The Man with the Dimples" and there was "The Girl with the Curls." But Norma would go to see any movie "The Vitagraph Girl" was in.

When "The Vitagraph Girl" laughed, Norma would sit in the dark and laugh. When the actress cried, the fan cried. Norma just knew she would be on that screen someday in a movie with her idol — "The Vitagraph Girl." She just knew she had to do it.

❖ Chapter 3 ❖
Don't Call Us— We'll Call You!

Norma spent so much time at the movies and so much time making believe she was a star that she forgot a few other important things. One was school, and that caught up with her one day. It was late afternoon. Norma and Peg were sitting on the front porch.

"Norma," her mother said suddenly. "Did you cut school again today?"

What could Norma say? It was no use trying to lie to Peg. Slowly, she told the truth. She had been going to Prospect Park at least once a week. With a group of other children, she hid her schoolbooks in the bushes and played theatre.

"You don't seem to show much interest in school, Norma," Peg said. "In fact the higher you go in school, the lower your marks become. It seems to me," her mother went on, "there isn't any point in our pinching every penny, saving just to keep you in school. Perhaps you'd better give up high school. You'll have to decide on some way of making a living sooner or later, anyhow. It might as well be now. Do you have any ideas?"

Norma didn't know what to say. She and Peg sat looking at each other for quite a while. Finally Peg spoke again in her quiet way.

"Norma, how would like to go into moving pictures?"

"Oh," said the surprised Norma, "more than anything in the world, Peg. You know that! But how could I?"

"The usual way to start anything is to try," her mother answered. Then she smiled for the first time and reached for Norma's hand.

The very next day Peg and Norma boarded the Brooklyn Rapid Transit elevated train. They were headed for the Vitagraph Film Studio. It was three miles away in a quiet farm area in Brooklyn. And that's where most movies were made in the early 1900s.

At this point a surprised Shaun Cassidy broke into Lola Pearsons's story. "Movies were made in Brooklyn? Where was Hollywood in those days, Lola?"

"Right where it is today, Shaun. But it was a tiny town near Los Angeles that few people had ever heard about," Lola answered.

Peg thought Norma might get a part as an *extra*. This was the kind of job that would come up from time to time on a movie lot. A movie studio like Vitagraph would need to picture a crowd and they would use as many people as they could find. Often extras were just people who showed up at the studio that morning. They were paid between two and three dollars each.

"Did they know someone at the film studio? How did they get in?" Shaun asked.

Here is an early movie set at the Vitagraph Studios in Brooklyn.

"They didn't need to know anyone," answered Lola.

In those days the movie lot was not what it is today. Anyone who was good-looking and had the courage to show up at the studio was welcome to try out for a part. But the day Peg took Norma to Vitagraph all the extra parts had been given away.

"Shall I come back tomorrow?" Norma asked. She was told not to. They would write to her if there was a part she could play.

❖ Chapter 4 ❖

Norma and The Four-Footed Pest

No letter came from the studio. It had been just over a week, but to Norma it felt like a year. Then one morning Peg asked Norma to do some shopping for her. Norma was to keep a quarter for herself. She decided to use that money for a train to the Vitagraph Studio.

All on her own, without a word to Peg, Norma would try again for a job in the movies. She told only one person of her plan. It was "Baby," as everyone called her sister Constance. She asked Baby to go with her.

Deep down Norma had the feeling that perhaps the studio had not sent for her because they thought she looked too young. So she "borrowed" a rose-colored dress from Peg's closet and a wide picture hat with roses growing upside down over the left ear. Then

Norma tied her curls into two long braids. She wound them around her head and stuffed them under the hat. The mirror told her she looked like a woman of the world.

At the Vitagraph Studio, holding Baby by the hand, Norma approached the person at the desk. It was Mr. Sam Spedon of the publicity department. He looked at Norma and Baby for a while. If he wanted to laugh, he did not. He simply asked Norma what she did.

"I've posed for slides," Norma told him.

Just then Mrs. Breuill, who was in charge of writing movie stories, came by and stopped to talk to Mr. Spedon. Something about Mrs. Breuill's amused smile made Norma feel that her mirror had lied to her about how much older she looked. Could it be that she just looked funny?

She began to pull at the flowers on Peg's hat. And just then the worst thing happened! One of her braids came tumbling down over her face.

Mrs. Breuill reached over and took off Norma's hat. She untied the other braid. "There," she said. "How much better! Now you look like a human being, and we can probably use you. She has lovely eyes," she whispered to Mr. Spedon.

It was a good lesson for Norma, one she never forgot. She had learned that just being herself, not trying to be someone else, was the first step toward becoming an actress. Mrs. Breuill told Norma and Baby they could both stay.

On the set four or five films were being made at the same time. Men and women were dashing about dressed as knights, pirates, cowboys, queens, kings, and maids. And always a machine made a loud clicking sound. That was the camera. The set was a lot different from today's movie or TV set, where all is quiet, well-run, and the many cameras never make a sound.

All the noise and movement scared the life out of Norma! A friendly carpenter in blue overalls yanked Baby and Norma back. "Be careful," he warned. "They're gonna shoot!"

Norma and Baby covered their ears expecting a deafening noise. But they soon found out that "shoot" meant "start filming." After watching some of the "shooting," she and Baby were taken to the outdoor lot and put to work. Norma had her first movie job. She would be an extra in a movie called *The Four-Footed Pest*. It was about the adventures of a young horse that was always getting people into hot water. And Norma's part in the movie was to kiss a young photographer on a street corner.

In the story the photographer didn't want to be seen kissing a young girl on the street. He pulled his black camera cloth over both their heads. A horse would come along and lift the cloth with its teeth. There would be the back of Norma's head as she held her arms around the young man. Then she and the photographer both ran away.

That was Norma Talmadge's first scene in a movie. A picture of the back of her head.

It was a sad moment for her. Here she was in the movies, and no one could even see her face!

❖ Chapter 5 ❖
Norma Meets "The Vitagraph Girl"

"Norma's movie was finished in half a day, Shaun. The whole picture." "Man!" said Shaun. "A picture today can take six months or more. Even a one hour TV show can take weeks."

"You have to remember, Shaun, most movies then were only one reel—about 15 minutes playing time. And most of the time the stories were written the night before the movies were made."

Norma's biggest thrill that first day was when the wardrobe department gave her a costume to put on in place of Peg's clothes. The lady in charge of costumes — Mrs. Turner — was very nice to Norma. "Perhaps you will meet my daughter, Florence. She is a player

here at Vitagraph. In fact, they call her 'The Vitagraph Girl.' " Norma almost fell over! She had finally heard the name of her idol! "The Vitagraph Girl" was Florence Turner. And her mother was a . . . a costume lady?

Norma would soon learn that the movie actors and actresses had to do a lot more than act in the early movie days. They would make each other up, fix costumes, paint scenery, hammer sets together — anything and everything that had to be done.

One of the big stage stars then was an actor named Maurice Costello. He began to change things at the movie studios when he started to make movies. Mr. Costello would not use a hammer or a paintbrush. He was an actor, he said, not a handyman. But even the great Maurice Costello dressed in a room with seven or eight other actors. By the way, he was the star known to millions of people as "The Man with the Dimples."

The pretty Florence Turner, the female star of the studio, gave the extras their money each evening. At the end of her first day, Norma was given $2.50 for her services.

"Two and half dollars!" Shaun whistled. "I can't believe it. Sylvester Stallone just signed a contract for two million dollars for one feature!"

Mary Pickford, a star of the early 1900s, is *Pollyanna* carrying a lamp into the dark hall. Pickford went on to star in "talkies."

"But Sylvester Stallone never got his pay envelope handed to him by a star like Florence Turner," Lola laughed.

On her way out Norma asked at the desk when she should be back. "Don't come back until you're sent for," they told her. "You'll hear from us by mail."

All Norma could think about for the next weeks was when that letter might come from the studio. But each day there was no letter with the name Vitagraph Company in the upper left hand corner. Three weeks passed.

Then, in the middle of the fourth week, a loud whistle from the mailman brought Norma downstairs on the run. His hand held a special delivery letter. It was for Norma and it was from Vitagraph.

Norma Talmadge in the silent film, *Kiki*.

❖ Chapter 6 ❖
Life for the Vitagraph Stars

That letter answered all of Norma's hopes. It was a brief form letter asking her to be at the studio at nine o'clock the following morning. And to ask for Mr. Charles Kent, a movie director.

This time Peg went with her. It's lucky she did. Norma never could have stayed on her feet when Mr. Kent told her the news. She would play in a movie called *The Dixie Mother*. She would be the daughter of a southern mother during the American Civil War. Mr. Kent told her that the actress playing her mother would be none other than Florence Turner!

The movie film would be 900 feet — about ten minutes long. One camera would be used. Florence Turner sat between chalk marks on the floor. Everyone in the film had to stay between those marks.

Suddenly, Norma was called. She didn't move. She was frozen with fear. How could she be in a picture with "The Vitagraph Girl"? Mr. Kent was angry. He came up behind Norma and *pushed* her. And Norma was on camera, being held by her sobbing mother Florence Turner.

Norma worked in one movie or another every day for the next two weeks. She got five dollars for every day she worked. Soon Peg and Norma's sisters were used as extras. Times were getting a bit better for the Talmadge family.

There were about 100 players at Vitagraph. They all got about the same pay — from $25 to $35 a week. One day a player would star in a movie. The next day he would be an extra.

The men's dressing rooms were all on one side. The women's dressing rooms on the other. Only Florence Turner was allowed to use the president's office when she was tired. She could lie on the couch between scenes. To the rest of the actors, that seemed the life of a real star.

There were lots of problems for the stars in those early days of the movies. Once when Florence Turner was playing *Carmen,* the crowd in the bullring was painted on a piece of canvas. The wall suddenly came crashing down on one of the actors. In the same

Constance Talmadge, Norma's sister, also went ▶
on to become a movie star. Here she is *Cleopatra.*

picture another star had a problem. She was Viola, the Vitagraph cow. Viola was hired from a Brooklyn farmer at 25¢ a day. She played in all sorts of films with a country background.

But in *Carmen*, Viola had her roughest part to play. She would play a maddened bull in a bullring! First they wrapped Viola in three coats of canvas. Then she was painted black. Finally a pair of elk horns were glued to her head. As if this wasn't enough, paper "hair" was pasted between the horns. Sweet Viola stood all this quietly.

Then the big moment came. Viola was to charge into the bullring and rush at the toreador. But Viola wouldn't move. She didn't make a single move toward the toreador. In fact, she didn't even look at him. The director of the film, Mr. Blackton, ordered a shotgun fired behind her. Viola shot across the arena! The only trouble was she kept right on going. They got the picture just before the walls came tumbling down.

❖ Chapter 7 ❖
Norma Joins the Family

The actors at Vitagraph were really like one big happy family. No one ever thought of being snooty. Between scenes the stars chatted with the extras and nobody put on airs. Norma loved every minute of it. She played everything from children's parts to an old lady of 60. Whenever she had to look older they padded her clothes and put up her hair. She made all kinds of pictures, from slapstick comedy to historical dramas. Sometimes she made two pictures a day.

After some weeks the worst thing possible for Norma happened. She was "laid off." While she waited for a new movie she tried to figure out how she could get a full-time job at Vitagraph. It was all she could think about. After a long talk with Peg, she decided to go to the studio and make them let her try out for the acting staff. No more day-to-day parts for Norma!

46

Peg always said there was no harm in asking good questions, and to ask for steady work seemed about as good a question as there could be. So once again mother and daughter boarded the train and set out for the Vitagraph Studio.

There was always a long line waiting to see Mr. Smith and Mr. Blackton. Some wanted jobs. Others simply wanted to talk about their problems. But everybody wanted to see the bosses. Peg and Norma were way at the back of the line. But not for long!

Norma asked Peg to hold her place. Never looking back, she sailed past 20 or 30 other people to the head of the line.

"I'm a little late for my appointment. Would you mind letting me through? Mr. Smith is expecting me," she said with her sweetest smile.

It worked like magic and Norma walked right in. Mr. Smith remembered her right away. When she got back, Peg was still standing in line.

"Let's go. I have to get some sleep. I have to be back at nine in the morning. If I do well for two weeks I have a full-time job here."

Norma Talmadge was on her way. One day she would be the biggest star of the movies. And she would be known, not as any "Vitagraph Girl", but by her own name.

Lola Pearsons had stopped talking. Shaun Cassidy wished she had not. There was so much more he wanted to hear about those early stars of the movies. Suddenly there was a knock at the door.

"On the set, Mr. Cassidy. We are ready to shoot."

Shaun looked at Lola. "I think I know why you told me the story of Norma Talmadge. My life looks a lot better to me now. But I want to hear more. When can we have lunch again?"

Lola's eyes moved from Shaun to the tray of lunch that had never even been touched. She smiled. "Shaun, let's not make it for lunch next time. I'm afraid we'll both starve to death!"